I0887264

ALL YOUR FAVORITE Hats

10 Crochet & Knit Hat Projects

LEISURE ARTS, INC. • Maumelle, Arkansas

Contents

Bathgate Hat 4

Cabled Hat 8

Boys Ribbed Hat 12

Cabled Bun Hat. 16

Herringbone Hat 20

Wildwood Hat 24

Gisburn Forest Hat 28

Easy Slouch Hat 32

Meghan's Hat. 36

Urban Minimalist Hat 40

General Instructions. 44

LION BRAND® 24/7 COTTON

Bathgate Hat

EASY

SIZES

Finished Circumference:
About 19½ in. (49.5 cm), Hat will stretch to fit a range of sizes

Finished Height:
About 9 in. (23 cm)

GAUGE

16 sc = about 4 in. (10 cm).

BE SURE TO CHECK YOUR GAUGE.

MATERIALS

Yarn (Medium) MEDIUM 4

Lion Brand® 24/7 COTTON (Art. #761)

- ☐ #158 Goldenrod 1 ball (A)
- ☐ #172 Grass 1 ball (B)
- ☐ #110 Navy 1 ball (C)
- ☐ #142 Rose 1 ball (D)
- ☐ #178 Jade 1 ball (E)
- ☐ #144 Magenta 1 ball (F) or colors of your choice
- ☐ Lion Brand® crochet hook size H-8 (5 mm)
- ☐ Lion Brand® stitch markers
- ☐ Lion Brand® large-eyed blunt needle

NOTES

1. Hat is worked in one piece in continuous rnds.
2. The yarn color is changed to make stripes.
3. To change yarn color, work last st of old color to last yarn over. Yarn over with new color and draw through all loops to complete st. Fasten off old color. Proceed with new color.

HAT

With A, ch 2.

Work 6 sc in the first ch; join with sl st in first sc – 6 sc.

Place marker for beginning of rnd and move marker up as each rnd is completed.

Rnd 1: Work 2 sc in each sc around – you will have 12 sc at the end of Rnd 1.

Rnd 2: *Work 2 sc in next sc, sc in next sc; rep from * around – 18 sc.

Rnd 3: *Work 2 sc in next sc, sc in next 2 sc; rep from * around – 24 sc.

Rnd 4: *Work 2 sc in next sc, sc in next 3 sc; rep from * around – 30 sc.

Rnd 5: *Work 2 sc in next sc, sc in next 4 sc; rep from * around – 36 sc.

Rnd 6: *Work 2 sc in next sc, sc in next 5 sc; rep from * around– 42 sc.

Rnd 7: *Work 2 sc in next sc, sc in next 6 sc; rep from * around – 48 sc.

Rnd 8: *Work 2 sc in next sc, sc in next 7 sc; rep from * around – 54 sc.

Rnd 9: *Work 2 sc in next sc, sc in next 8 sc; rep from * around – 60 sc.

Rnd 10: *Work 2 sc in next sc, sc in next 9 sc; rep from * around – 66 sc.

Rnd 11: *Work 2 sc in the next sc, sc in next 10 sc; rep from * around – 72 sc.

Rnd 12: *Work 2 sc in the next sc, sc in next 11 sc; rep from * around, changing to B in the last st – 78 sc.

Rnd 13: With B, and working in back loops only, sc in each sc around.

Rnds 14-19: With B, sc in each sc around, changing to C in the last st of Rnd 19.

Rnds 20-26: With C, sc in each sc around, changing to D in the last st of Rnd 26.

Rnds 27-33: With D, sc in each sc around, changing to E in the last st of Rnd 33.

Rnds 34-36: With E, sc in each sc around, changing to F in the last st of Rnd 36.

Rnds 37-42: With F, sc in each sc around, changing to C in the last st of Rnd 42.

Rnd 43: With C, *2 sc in next sc, sc in next 2 sc; rep from * around – 104 sc.

Rnds 44-49: With C, sc in each sc around, changing to A in the last st of Rnd 49.

Rnd 50: With A, *2 sc in next sc, sc in next 2 sc; rep from * to last 2 sc, sc in last 2 sc – 138 sc.

Rnd 51: With A, sc in each sc around.

Join with sl st in first sc and fasten off.

FINISHING

Weave in ends.

LION BRAND® HOMETOWN USA®

Cabled Hat

●●○○ **EASY**

SIZES

Finished Circumference:
About 20 in. (51 cm), will stretch to fit a range of sizes

Finished Length:
About 8½ in. (21.5 cm)

GAUGE

11 sts + 10 rows = about 4 in. (10 cm) in Cable pattern.

BE SURE TO CHECK YOUR GAUGE.

MATERIALS

Yarn (Super Bulky) SUPER BULKY 6

Lion Brand® HOMETOWN USA® (Art. #135)

- ☐ # 149 Dallas Gray 1 ball
- ☐ Lion Brand® cable needle
- ☐ Lion Brand® stitch markers
- ☐ Lion Brand® large-eyed blunt needle

Additional Materials

Double pointed knitting needles size 13 (9 mm), set of 4 or 5

NOTES

1. Hat is worked in one piece on double pointed needles.

STITCH EXPLANATIONS

2/2 LC (2 over 2 left cross) Slip 2 sts to cable needle and hold in front of work, k2, then k2 from cable needle.

1/1 LC (1 over 1 left cross) Slip 1 st to cable needle and hold in front of work, k1, then k1 from cable needle.

ssk (slip, slip, knit) Slip next 2 sts as if to knit, one at a time, to right needle; insert left needle into fronts of these 2 sts and knit them tog – 1 st decreased.

HAT

Cast on 54 sts, dividing sts as evenly as possible onto 3 or 4 double pointed needles. Place marker for beg of rnd. Join by working the first st on the left hand needle with the working yarn from the right hand needle and being careful not to twist sts.

Rnds 1, 2, and 4: * P2, k4; rep from * around.

Rnd 3: *P2, 2/2 LC; rep from * around.

Rnds 5-16: Rep Rnds 1-4.

Rnds 17 and 18: Rep Rnds 1 and 2.

Rnd 19: *P2, sl next 2 sts to cable needle (cn) and hold in front of work, k2tog, then k2 from cn; rep from * around – 45 sts at the end of this rnd.

Rnd 20: *P2, k3; rep from * around.

Rnd 21: *P2, sl next st to cn and hold in front of work, k2tog, then k1 from cn; rep from * around – 36 sts.

Rnd 22: *P2, k2; rep from * around.

Rnd 23: *P2tog, sl next st to cn and hold in front of work, k1, then k1 from cn; rep from * around – 27 sts.

Rnd 24: *P1, k2; rep from * around.

Rnd 25: *P1, ssk; rep from * around – 18 sts.

Rnd 26: *P1, k1; rep from * around.

Rnd 27: *K2tog; rep from * around – 9 sts.

Rnd 28: Knit.

Cut yarn, leaving a long yarn tail. Thread through remaining sts, draw tightly together and knot to secure.

FINISHING

Weave in ends.

LION BRAND® JEANS®

Boys Ribbed Hat

●●○○ **EASY**

SIZES

Finished Circumference:
About 15 in. (38 cm), will stretch to fit a range of sizes

GAUGE

25 sts = about 4 in. (10 cm) in k2, p2 rib slightly stretched

BE SURE TO CHECK YOUR GAUGE.

MATERIALS

Yarn (Medium) MEDIUM 4
Lion Brand® JEANS® (Art. #505)

- ☐ #109 Stonewash 1 ball
- ☐ Lion Brand® double pointed needles size 6 (4 mm)
- ☐ Lion Brand® stitch markers
- ☐ Lion Brand® large-eyed blunt needle

Additional Materials
Circular knitting needle size 6 (4 mm), 16 in. (40.5 cm) long

NOTES

1. Hat is worked in one piece in the round, beginning on a circular needle then changing to double-pointed needles.
2. Top of Hat is shaped by working simple decreases.

HAT

With circular needle, cast on 92 sts. Place marker for beg of rnd. Join by working the first st on the left hand needle with the working yarn from the right hand needle and being careful not to twist sts.

Rnd 1: *K2, p2; rep from * around.

Rep Rnd 1 until piece measures about 10 in. (25.5 cm) from beginning.

Shape Top of Hat

Note: When working Rnd 1, you'll be decreasing sts. Change to double-pointed needles as you work Rnd 1. Be sure to move your st marker onto the double-pointed needles as well!

Rnd 1: *K2, p2tog; rep from * to end of round – you will have 69 sts.

Rnd 2: K the knit sts and p the purl sts around.

Rnd 3: *K2tog, p1; rep from * around – 46 sts.

Rnd 4: Rep Rnd 2.

Rnd 5: K2tog around – 23 sts.

Rnd 6: Knit.

Cut yarn, leaving a long yarn tail. Thread yarn tail into blunt needle, then draw through remaining sts. Pull to close top of Hat, then knot.

FINISHING

Weave in ends.

LION BRAND® SCARFIE®

Cabled Bun Hat

●●○○ **EASY**

SIZES

Finished Circumference:
About 20 in. (51 cm), will stretch to fit a range of sizes

Finished Height:
About 6 in. (15 cm)

GAUGE

32 sts = about 4 in. (10 cm) over Rows 1-4 of pattern.

BE SURE TO CHECK YOUR GAUGE.

MATERIALS

Yarn (Bulky) BULKY 5

Lion Brand® SCARFIE® (Art. #826)

- ☐ #216 Cream/Silver 1 ball
- ☐ Lion Brand® knitting needles size 7 (4.5 mm)
- ☐ Lion Brand® double pointed knitting needles size 7 (4.5 mm)
- ☐ Lion Brand® cable needle
- ☐ Lion Brand® large-eyed blunt needle

NOTES

1. Hat is worked in one piece and then seamed.
2. The top of the Hat is open.
3. Yarn overs are worked every 4 rows to create eyelets. A knitted cord is worked separately, then woven through the eyelets to shape the top of the Hat.

STITCH EXPLANATIONS

2/2 LC (2 over 2 left cross) Slip 2 sts to cable needle and hold in front, k2, then k2 from cable needle.

RT (Right Twist) K2tog and leave on left hand needle, then with right hand needle, go between the 2 sts and k the first st again.

Yo (yarn over)
An increase that also creates a small decorative hole (eyelet) in the fabric, worked as follows:

1. Bring yarn to front, between the needles.

2. Take yarn to back, over the right hand needle. This creates the new stitch. You are now ready to proceed with the next stitch as instructed.

HAT

With straight needles, cast on 48 sts.

Rows 1 and 3 (WS): K2, *p4, k2, p2, k2; rep from * to last 6 sts, p4, k2.

Row 2: K1, p1, *k4, p2, RT, p2; rep from * to last 6 sts, k4, p1, k1.

Row 4: K1, p1, *2/2 LC, p2, RT, p2; rep from * to last 16 sts, 2/2 LC, p2, RT, yo, p2tog, 2/2 LC, p1, k1.

Rep Rows 1-4 until piece measures about 20 in. (51 cm) from beginning, end with a Row 2 as the last row you work.

Bind off.

FINISHING

Sew ends of piece together to make a ring.

Knitted Cord
With 2 double pointed needles, cast on 3 sts. Knit the 3 sts. Do not turn work. *Slide sts to other end of needle and knit them, pulling yarn tightly across the back of the work, (do not turn work); rep from * until cord measures about 31 in. (78.5 cm) long.

Bind off.

Weave cord through the yarn over eyelets, then knot ends of cord together.

Weave in ends.

LION BRAND® WOOL-EASE®

Herringbone Hat

EASY

SIZES

Finished Circumference:
About 19 in. (48.5 cm), will stretch to fit a range of sizes

GAUGE

15 dc + 7 rnds = about 4 in. (10 cm).

BE SURE TO CHECK YOUR GAUGE.

MATERIALS

Yarn (Medium) 4

Lion Brand® WOOL-EASE® (Art. #620)

- ☐ #151 Grey Heather 1 ball (A)
- ☐ #152 Oxford Grey 1 ball (B)
- ☐ Lion Brand® crochet hook size H-8 (5 mm)
- ☐ Lion Brand® Pom Pom Maker
- ☐ Lion Brand® large-eyed blunt needle

Additional Materials

4 small buttons

Sewing needle and thread

NOTES

1. Hat is worked in one piece in the round with the right side always facing, beginning at top.
2. The pom pom is tied to completed Hat.
3. Buttons are decorative only.
4. When you see "– 12 sts" in the instructions, this lets you know how many sts you will have at the end of that specific row.

STITCH EXPLANATIONS

BPHDC (Back Post half double crochet) Yarn over, insert hook from back to front then to back again, going around post of indicated st, draw up a loop, yarn over and draw through all loops on hook. Skip st in front of the BPHDC.

FPHDC (Front Post half double crochet) Yarn over, insert hook from front to back then to front, going around post of indicated st, draw up a loop, yarn over and draw through all loops on hook. Skip st behind the FPHDC.

FPDC (Front Post double crochet) Yarn over, insert hook from front to back then to front, going around post of indicated st, draw up a loop, (yarn over and draw through 2 loops on hook) twice. Skip st behind the FPDC.

HAT

With A, ch 4; join with sl st to form a ring.

Rnd 1: Ch 2 (does not count as a st in this rnd and all following rnds), work 11 dc in ring; join with sl st in top of beg ch.

Rnd 2: Ch 2, (dc, FPDC) in each st around (first work the dc, then work the FPDC around the same st); join with sl st in top of beg ch – you will have 22 sts.

Rnd 3: Ch 2, *(FPDC, dc) in next st (first work the FPDC, then work the dc behind it), (dc, FPDC) in next st (first work the dc, then work the FPDC around the same st); rep from * around; join with sl st in top of beg ch – 44 sts.

Rnd 4: Ch 2, *sk next FPDC, (FPDC, dc) in next dc, (dc, FPDC) in next dc, sk next FPDC; rep from * around; join with sl st in top of beg ch.

Rnd 5: Ch 2, *sk next FPDC, (FPDC, 2 dc) in next dc, (2 dc, FPDC) in next dc, sk next FPDC; rep from * around; join with sl st in top of beg ch – 66 sts.

Rnd 6: Ch 2, *sk next FPDC, (FPDC, 2 dc) in next dc, dc in next 2 dc, (2 dc, FPDC) in next dc, sk next FPDC; rep from * around; join with sl st in top of beg ch – 88 sts.

Rnd 7: Ch 2, *sk next FPDC, sk next dc, (FPDC, 2 dc) in next dc, dc in next 2 dc, (2 dc, FPDC) in next dc, sk next dc, sk next FPDC; rep from * around; join with sl st in top of beg ch – 88 sts.

Rep Rnd 7 until Hat measures about 7½ in. (19 cm) from beginning.

Next Rnd (Decrease Rnd): Ch 2, *sk next FPDC, sk next dc, (FPDC, dc) in next dc, dc in next 2 dc, (dc, FPDC) in next dc, sk next dc, sk next FPDC; rep from * around; join with sl st in top of beg ch – 66 sts.

Do NOT fasten off.

Band

Rnd 1: Ch 1, *FPHDC in next FPDC, BPHDC in next dc, FPHDC in next 2 dc, BPHDC in next dc, FPHDC in next FPDC; rep from * around; join with sl st to beg ch – 66 sts.

Rnd 2: Ch 1, *FPHDC, BPHDC, (FPHDC) twice, BPHDC, FPHDC; rep from * around; join with sl st to beg ch.

Rnds 3-10: Rep Rnd 2 for 8 more times.

Fasten off.

FINISHING

Weave in ends.

With B and following package instructions, make a pom pom. Tie pom pom to top of Hat.

With sewing needle and thread, sew buttons to band.

LION BRAND® WOOL-EASE® THICK & QUICK®

Wildwood Hat

EASY

SIZES

Finished Circumference: About 20 in. (51 cm), will stretch to fit a range of sizes

GAUGE

5 pattern reps = about 4½ in. (11.5 cm) over Rows 1-6 of pattern.

Note: One pattern rep consists of a ch-1 sp and the following sc.

BE SURE TO CHECK YOUR GAUGE.

MATERIALS

Yarn (Super Bulky) SUPER BULKY 6

Lion Brand® WOOL-EASE® THICK & QUICK® (Art. #640)

- ☐ #612 Coney Island 2 balls
- ☐ Lion Brand® crochet hook size N-13 (9 mm)
- ☐ Lion Brand® Pom-Pom Maker
- ☐ Lion Brand® large-eyed blunt needle

NOTES

1. Hat is worked in joined and turned rnds beginning at lower edge.
2. If you find it difficult to join the beg ch into a ring without twisting the ch, Rnd 1 can be worked as a row, then joined into a rnd, as follows: Leaving a long beg tail, ch 45, sc in 2nd ch from hook, *ch 1, sk next ch, sc in next ch; rep from * to last ch, ch 1, sk last ch; join with sl st in first sc – you will have 22 pattern reps (22 sc and 22 ch-1 sps) in this row/rnd. Use beg tail to sew gap at base of first row closed. Proceed to Rnd 2.
3. For those who find a visual helpful, we have included a stitch diagram.

HAT

Ch 44; taking care not to twist ch, join with sl st in first ch to form a ring.

Rnd 1 (WS): Ch 1, sc in same ch as join, *ch 1, sk next ch, sc in next ch; rep from * to last ch, ch 1, sk last ch; join with sl st in first ch – you will have 22 pattern reps (22 sc and 22 ch-1 sps) in this rnd.

Rnds 2-6: Ch 1, turn, sc in first ch-1 sp, *ch 1, sk next sc, sc in next ch-1 sp; rep from * to last sc, ch 1, sk last sc; join with sl st in first ch.

Rnd 7 (WS): Ch 3, turn, dc in first ch-1 sp (beg ch-3 and first dc count as first 2-dc group), 2 dc in each ch-1 sp around; join with sl st in top of beg ch-3 – Twenty-two 2-dc groups.

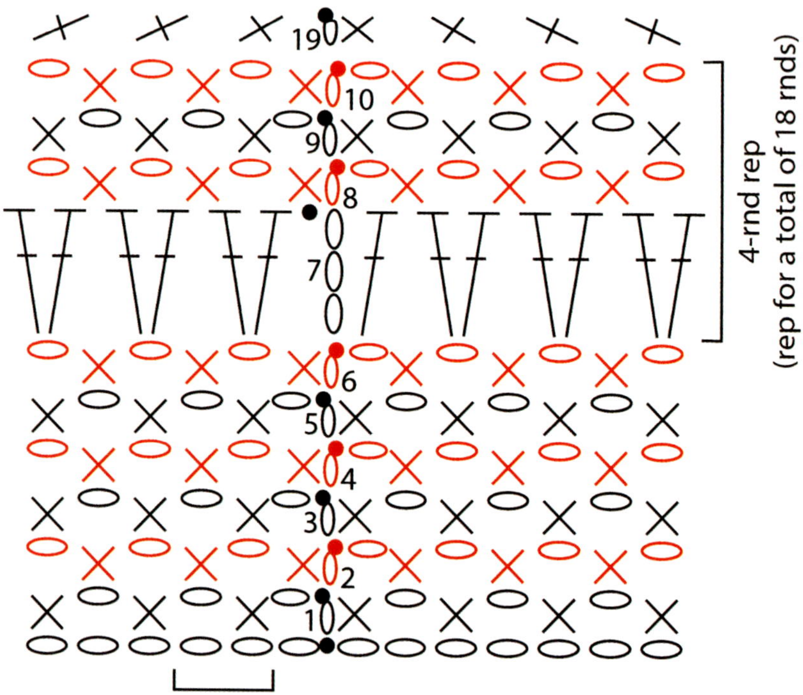

pattern rep
(rep all the way around)

KEY

● = slip stitch (sl st)

⬭ = chain (ch)

✕ = single crochet (sc)

= double crochet (dc)

Rnd 8: Ch 1, turn, sc in sp before first 2-dc group, *ch 1, sc in next sp between 2-dc groups; rep from * around, ch 1; join with sl st in first ch – 22 sc and 22 ch-1 sps.

Rnds 9 and 10: Rep Rnd 2 twice.

Rnds 11-18: Rep Rnds 7-10 twice.

Rnd 19 (Decrease Rnd): Ch 1, turn, sc in each ch-1 sp around; join with sl st in first ch – 22 sc.

Fasten off, leaving a long yarn tail. Thread yarn tail into blunt needle and through sts of last rnd. Pull tail to close opening at top of Hat and knot.

FINISHING

Pom-Pom

Following package directions, make a large pom-pom. Tie pom-pom to top of Hat.

Weave in yarn ends.

LION BRAND® TOUCH OF ALPACA™

Gisburn Forest Hat

●●●○ **INTERMEDIATE**

SIZES

Circumference:
About 16½ in. (42 cm), will stretch to fit a range of sizes

Height:
About 8 in. (20.5 cm)

GAUGE

24 sts + 30 rnds = about 4 in. (10 cm) over Rnds 1–8 of Cable pattern.

BE SURE TO CHECK YOUR GAUGE.

MATERIALS

MEDIUM 4

Yarn (Medium)
Lion Brand® TOUCH OF ALPACA™ (Art. #674)

- ☐ #123 Taupe 1 ball
- ☐ Lion Brand® double pointed knitting needles size 8 (5 mm)
- ☐ Lion Brand® cable needles
- ☐ Lion Brand® stitch markers
- ☐ Lion Brand® stitch holders
- ☐ Lion Brand® Pom-Pom Maker
- ☐ Lion Brand® large-eyed blunt needle

Additional Materials
Circular knitting needle size 8 (5 mm), 16 in. (40.5 cm) long

NOTES

1. Earflaps are worked separately, back and forth in rows, from lower point upwards. Sts are cast-on between Earflaps for Hat, then Hat is worked in the round.
2. The Cable pattern can be worked by following the written instructions or by reading the chart. Read Cable chart from right to left on all rounds.
3. Pom-poms are worked separately, then tied to top of Hat.

STITCH EXPLANATIONS

2/2 LC (2 over 2 left cross) Slip 2 sts to cable needle and hold in front of work, k2, then k2 from cable needle.

2/2 RC (2 over 2 right cross) Slip 2 sts to cable needle and hold in back of work, k2, then k2 from cable needle.

EARFLAPS *(Make 2)*

Cord

With 2 double pointed needles, cast on 3 sts.

Knit the 3 sts. Do not turn work. *Slide sts to other end of needle and knit them, pulling yarn tightly across the back of the work, (do not turn work); rep from * until cord measures about 8 in. (20.5 cm) long.

Earflap

Row 1 (RS): K1, (k1, p1, k1) all into next st, k1 – you will have 5 sts in this row.

Row 2: P1, (k1, p1) twice.

Row 3: K1, p1, (k1, p1, k1) all into next st, p1, k1 – 7 sts.

Row 4: P1, k1, p3, k1, p1.

Row 5: K1, p1, k1, (k1, p1, k1) all into next st, k1, p1, k1 – 9 sts.

Row 6: P1, k1, p2, place marker, p3, k1, p1.

Row 7: K1, p1, k to marker, slip marker, (k1, p1, k1) into next st, k to last 2 sts, p1, k1 – 11 sts.

Row 8: P1, k1, p to last 2 sts, k1, p1, slipping marker as you come to it.

Rows 9-20: Rep Rows 7 and 8 for 6 more times – 23 sts in Row 20.

Place sts on a st holder and remove the marker.

Set piece aside.

HAT

With circular needle, cast on 16 sts, k23 Earflap sts from one holder, cast on 30 sts for front of Hat, k23 Earflap sts from 2nd holder, cast on 16 sts for back of Hat.

Place a marker for beg of rnd. Join by knitting the first st on the left hand needle with the working yarn from the right hand needle and being careful not to twist sts – 108 sts.

Cable Pattern

Rnds 1-3: *K8, p4; rep from * to end of rnd.

Rnd 4: *2/2 LC, 2/2 RC, p4; rep from * to end of rnd.

Rnds 5-7: *K8, p4; rep from * to end of rnd.

Rnd 8: *2/2 LC, 2/2 RC, p4, 2/2 RC, 2/2 LC, p4, 2/2 LC, 2/2 RC, p4; rep from * to end of rnd.

Rnds 9-40: Rep Rnds 1-8 for 4 more times.

Shape Crown (top of Hat)

Note: When the number of sts no longer fit comfortably on the circular needle, change to double pointed needles.

Rnd 1: *K2tog, p1, (k1, p1) 3 times; rep from * to end of rnd – 96 sts.

Rnd 2: *K1, p1; rep from * to end of rnd.

Rnd 3: *K2tog, (k1, p1) 3 times; rep from * to end of rnd – 84 sts.

Rnd 4: *K2, p1, (k1, p1) twice; rep from * to end of rnd.

Rnd 5: *K2tog, p1, (k1, p1) twice; rep from * to end of rnd – 72 sts.

Rnd 6: *K1, p1; rep from * to end of rnd.

Rnd 7: *K2tog, (k1, p1) twice; rep from * to end of rnd – 60 sts.

Rnd 8: *K2, p1, k1, p1; rep from * to end of rnd.

Rnd 9: *K2tog, p1, k1, p1; rep from * to end of rnd – 48 sts.

Rnd 10: *K1, p1; rep from * to end of rnd.

Rnd 11: *K2tog, k1, p1; rep from * to end of rnd – 36 sts.

Rnd 12: *K2, p1; rep from * to end of rnd.

Rnd 13: *K2tog, p1; rep from * to end of rnd – 24 sts.

Rnd 14: *K1, p1; rep from * to end of rnd.

Rnd 15: K2tog around – 12 sts.

Cut yarn, leaving a long tail. Thread tail through remaining sts. Pull tail to close opening at top of Hat. Knot securely.

FINISHING

Pom-Poms

Following package directions, make 2 large pom-poms.

Tie pom-poms to top of Hat.

Tassels

Cut 14 strands of yarn, 6 in. (15 cm) long. Set 2 strands aside for ties. Thread 6 strands of yarn through the end of one Earflap cord. Fold in half and hold the strands in a bunch. Wrap and knot one tie around the strands about ½ in. (13 mm) below the end of the Earflap cord. Draw the ends of the wrap to the inside of the tassel. Rep to make a tassel on end of 2nd Earflap cord.

Weave in ends.

Cable Pattern

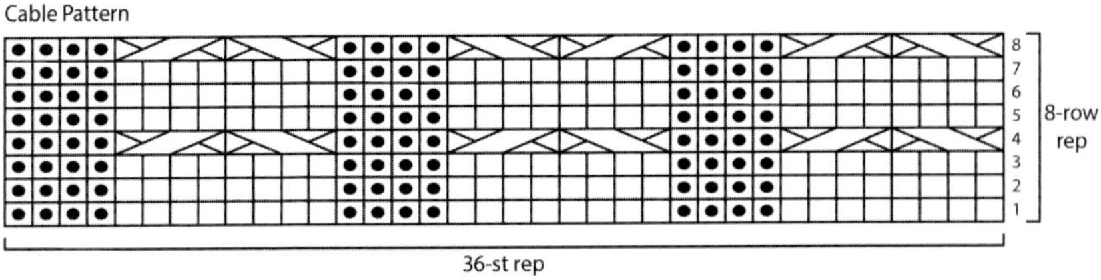

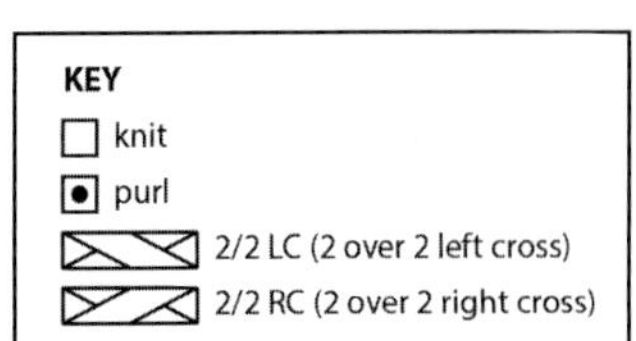

LION BRAND® HEARTLAND®

Easy Slouch Hat

●●○○ **EASY**

SIZES

Finished Circumference:
About 18 in. (45.5 cm), Hat will stretch to fit a range of sizes

Finished Length:
About 12 in. (30.5 cm)

GAUGE

16 sts = 4 in. (10 cm) over Rnds 1-10.

BE SURE TO CHECK YOUR GAUGE.

MATERIALS

Yarn (Medium) 4 MEDIUM

Lion Brand® HEARTLAND® (Art. #136)

- ☐ #176 Saguaro 1 ball
- ☐ Lion Brand® double pointed knitting needles size 9 (5.5 mm)
- ☐ Lion Brand® stitch markers
- ☐ Lion Brand® large-eyed blunt needle

Additional Materials

Circular knitting needle size 9 (5.5 mm), 16 in. (40.5 cm) long

NOTES

1. Hat is worked in one piece in the round, beginning on a circular needle then changing to double pointed needles when stitches have been sufficiently decreased.
2. The edge of the Hat is designed to roll slightly to the right side.

HAT

With circular needle, cast on 72 sts. Place a marker for beg of rnd. Join by knitting the first st on the left hand needle with the working yarn from the right hand needle and being careful not to twist sts.

Edge

Knit 5 rnds.

Rib Rnd: *K2, p2; rep from * around.

Rep Rib Rnd for 6 more times.

Body of Hat

Rnds 1-8: Knit.

Rnds 9 and 10: Purl.

Rep Rnds 1-10 for 5 more times.

Shape Crown (top of Hat)

Rnd 1 (Decrease Rnd): *K10, k2tog; rep from * around – you will have 66 sts.

Rnd 2: Knit.

Note: As you work Rnd 3, change to double pointed needles.

Rnd 3 (Decrease Rnd): *K9, k2tog; rep from * around – 60 sts.

Rnd 4: Knit.

Rnd 5 (Decrease Rnd): *K8, k2tog; rep from * around – 54 sts.

Rnd 6: Knit.

Rnd 7 (Decrease Rnd): *K7, k2tog; rep from * around – 48 sts.

Rnd 8: Knit.

Rnds 9 and 10: Purl.

Rnd 11 (Decrease Rnd): *K6, k2tog; rep from * around – 42 sts.

Rnd 12: Knit.

Rnd 13 (Decrease Rnd): *K5, k2tog; rep from * around – 36 sts.

Rnd 14: Knit.

Rnd 15 (Decrease Rnd): *K4, k2tog; rep from * around – 30 sts.

Rnd 16: Knit.

Rnd 17 (Decrease Rnd): *K2tog; rep from * around – 15 sts.

Cut yarn, leaving a long yarn tail. Thread tail into blunt needle. Draw needle through remaining sts and pull to gather. Knot securely.

FINISHING

Weave in ends.

LION BRAND® COLOR MADE EASY

Meghan's Hat

EASY

SIZES

Finished Circumference:
About 16 in. (40.5 cm), will stretch to fit a range of sizes

Finished Height:
About 10 in. (25.5 cm)

GAUGE

17 sts = about 4 in. (10 cm) in St st worked in the rnd (knit every rnd).

BE SURE TO CHECK YOUR GAUGE.

MATERIALS

Yarn (Bulky) 5 BULKY

Lion Brand® COLOR MADE EASY (Art. #195)

- ☐ #147 Ultra Violet 1 ball
- ☐ LION BRAND® size 10 (6 mm) double pointed knitting needles
- ☐ Lion Brand® large-eyed blunt needle

Additional Materials

Circular knitting needle size 10 (6 mm), 16 in. (40.5 cm) long

NOTES

1. Hat is worked in one piece in the round, beginning on a circular needle then changing to double-pointed needles.
2. Top of Hat is shaped by working simple decreases.
3. You can turn the ribbed edge of the Hat up to make a cuff, or uncuff it for a slouchy look.

STITCH EXPLANATION

ssk (slip, slip, knit) Slip next 2 sts as if to knit, one at a time, to right needle; insert left needle into fronts of these 2 sts and knit them together – 1 st decreased.

HAT

With circular needle, cast on 68 sts. Place marker for beg of rnd. Join by working the first st on the left hand needle with the working yarn from the right hand needle and being careful not to twist sts.

Ribbed Edge

Rnd 1: *K2, p2; repeat from * around.

Repeat Rnd 1 until piece measures about 4½ in. (11.5 cm) from beg.

Next Rnd: K2tog, knit 32, k2tog, knit to end of rnd – you'll have 66 sts.

Continue in St st worked in rnds (knit every rnd) and work until piece measures about 8 in. (20.5 cm) from beg.

Shape Top of Hat

Notes: On the next rnd, you'll be placing st markers for the decreases used to shape the top of the Hat. We suggest you use different color markers than the beg of rnd marker.

Change from circular needle to double-pointed needles when sts have been sufficiently decreased.

Don't forget to move your markers!

Set up Rnd: *Knit 22, place marker; repeat from * once more, knit to end of rnd.

Decrease for top of Hat

Rnd 1: *Ssk, knit to 3 sts before next marker, k2tog, k1, slip marker; repeat from * once more, ssk, knit to 3 sts before last marker, k2tog, k1.

Rnd 2: Knit.

Repeat Rnds 1 and 2 for 5 more times, then repeat Rnd 1 until you have 6 sts remaining between markers.

Last Rnd: *K2tog; repeat from * around – you'll have 9 sts.

Cut yarn, leaving a long yarn tail. Thread yarn tail into blunt needle, then draw through remaining sts. Pull to close top of Hat, then knot.

FINISHING

Weave in ends.

LION BRAND® FLIKKA

Urban Minimalist Hat

EASY

SIZES

Finished Circumference:
About 18 in. (45.5 cm), will stretch to fit a range of sizes

Finished Height:
About 12 in. (30.5 cm)

GAUGE

12 dc = about 4 in. (10 cm).

BE SURE TO CHECK YOUR GAUGE.

MATERIALS

Yarn (Light) 3 LIGHT
Lion Brand® FLIKKA (Art. #431)

- ☐ #704 Library Book 1 ball
- ☐ LION BRAND® crochet hook size J-10 (6 mm)
- ☐ Lion Brand® large-eyed blunt needle

NOTES

1. Hat is crocheted in one piece and then seamed.

STITCH EXPLANATION

dc2tog (double crochet 2 sts together) (Yarn over, insert hook in next st and draw up a loop, yarn over and draw through 2 loops) twice, yarn over and draw through all 3 loops on hook – 1 st decreased.

HAT

Ch 55.

Row 1: Sc in 2nd ch from hook and in each ch across – at the end of Row 1 you will have 54 sc.

Rows 2-4: Ch 1, turn, sc in each st across.

Row 5: Ch 3 (counts as first dc), turn, skip first st, dc in next st and in each st across.

Rep last row until piece measures about 11 in. (28 cm) from beginning.

Decrease Row: Ch 3 (does not count as first dc), turn, (dc2tog) across – you will have 27 sts.

Next Row: Ch 3 (counts as first dc), turn, skip first st, dc in next st and in each st across.

Fasten off, leaving a long yarn tail.

Thread tail into blunt needle and draw through sts of last row. Pull to gather and knot securely.

FINISHING

Seam sides of piece to make Hat.

Weave in ends.

General Instructions

ABBREVIATIONS

beg	begin(ning)
BPHDC	Back Post half double crochet(s)
ch(s)	chain(s)
cm	centimeters
cn	cable needle
dc	double crochet(s)
dc2tog	double crochet 2 together
FPDC	Front Post double crochet(s)
FPHDC	Front Post half double crochet(s)
K	knit
K2tog	knit 2 together
LC	left cross
mm	millimeters
P	purl
P2tog	purl 2 together
RC	right cross
rep(s)	repeat(s)
Rnd(s)	round(s)
RS	right side
RT	right twist
sc	single crochet(s)
sk	skip
sl	slip
sl st	slip stitch
sp(s)	space(s)
SSK	slip, slip, knit
st(s)	stitch(es)
St st	Stockinette stitch
tog	together
WS	wrong side
YO	yarn over

KNIT TERMINOLOGY		
UNITED STATES		INTERNATIONAL
gauge	=	tension
bind off	=	cast off
yarn over (YO)	=	yarn forward (yfwd) **or** yarn around needle (yrn)

CROCHET TERMINOLOGY		
UNITED STATES		INTERNATIONAL
slip stitch (slip st)	=	single crochet (sc)
single crochet (sc)	=	double crochet (dc)
half double crochet (hdc)	=	half treble crochet (htr)
double crochet (dc)	=	treble crochet (tr)
treble crochet (tr)	=	double treble crochet (dtr)
double treble crochet (dtr)	=	triple treble crochet (ttr)
triple treble crochet (tr tr)	=	quadruple treble crochet (qtr)
skip	=	miss

KNITTING NEEDLES		
UNITED STATES	ENGLISH U.K.	METRIC (mm)
0	13	2
1	12	2.25
2	11	2.75
3	10	3.25
4	9	3.5
5	8	3.75
6	7	4
7	6	4.5
8	5	5
9	4	5.5
10	3	6
10½	2	6.5
11	1	8
13	00	9
15	000	10
17	---	12.75
19	---	15
35	---	19
50	---	25

CROCHET HOOKS	
U.S.	Metric mm
B-1	2.25
C-2	2.75
D-3	3.25
E-4	3.5
F-5	3.75
G-6	4
7	4.5
H-8	5
I-9	5.5
J-10	6
K-10½	6.5
L-11	8
M/N-13	9
N/P-15	10
P/Q	15
Q	16
S	19

●○○○ **BASIC**	Projects using basic stitches. May include basic increases and decreases.
●●○○ **EASY**	Projects may include simple stitch patterns, color work, and/or shaping.
●●●○ **INTERMEDIATE**	Projects may include involved stitch patterns, color work, and/or shaping.
●●●● **COMPLEX**	Projects may include complex stitch patterns, color work, and/or shaping using a variety of techniques and stitches simultaneously.

■□□□ **BASIC**	Projects using basic stitches. May include basic increases and decreases.
■■□□ **EASY**	Projects may include simple stitch patterns, color work, and/or shaping.
■■■□ **INTERMEDIATE**	Projects may include involved stitch patterns, color work, and/or shaping.
■■■■ **COMPLEX**	Projects may include complex stitch patterns, color work, and/or shaping using a variety of techniques and stitches simultaneously.

Yarn Weight Symbol & Names	LACE 0	SUPER FINE 1	FINE 2	LIGHT 3	MEDIUM 4	BULKY 5	SUPER BULKY 6	JUMBO 7
Type of Yarns in Category	Fingering, size 10 crochet thread	Sock, Fingering, Baby	Sport, Baby	DK, Light Worsted	Worsted, Afghan, Aran	Chunky, Craft, Rug	Super Bulky, Roving	Jumbo, Roving
Knit Gauge Ranges in Stockinette St to 4" (10 cm)	33-40 sts**	27-32 sts	23-26 sts	21-24 sts	16-20 sts	12-15 sts	7-11 sts	6 sts and fewer
Advised Needle Size Range	000 to 1	1 to 3	3 to 5	5 to 7	7 to 9	9 to11	11 to 17	17 and larger

* GUIDELINES ONLY: The chart above reflects the most commonly used gauges and needle sizes for specific yarn categories.

** Lace weight yarns are usually knitted on larger needles to create lacy openwork patterns. Accordingly, a gauge range is difficult to determine. Always follow the gauge stated in your pattern.

Yarn Weight Symbol & Names	LACE 0	SUPER FINE 1	FINE 2	LIGHT 3	MEDIUM 4	BULKY 5	SUPER BULKY 6	JUMBO 7
Type of Yarns in Category	Fingering, size 10 crochet thread	Sock, Fingering, Baby	Sport, Baby	DK, Light Worsted	Worsted, Afghan, Aran	Chunky, Craft, Rug	Super Bulky, Roving	Jumbo, Roving
Crochet Gauge* Ranges in Single Crochet to 4" (10 cm)	32-42 sts**	21-32 sts	16-20 sts	12-17 sts	11-14 sts	8-11 sts	6-9 sts	5 sts and fewer
Advised Hook Size Range	Steel*** 6 to 8, Regular hook B-1	B-1 to E-4	E-4 to 7	7 to I-9	I-9 to K-10½	K-10½ to M/N-13	M/N-13 to Q	Q and larger

*GUIDELINES ONLY: The chart above reflects the most commonly used gauges and hook sizes for specific yarn categories.

** Lace weight yarns are usually crocheted with larger hooks to create lacy openwork patterns. Accordingly, a gauge range is difficult to determine. Always follow the gauge stated in your pattern.

SYMBOLS & TERMS

* — work instructions following * as many **more** times as indicated in addition to the first time.

( ) or **[ ]** — work enclosed instructions **as many** times as specified by the number immediately following **or** work all enclosed instructions in the stitch or space indicated **or** contains explanatory remarks.

GAUGE

Exact gauge is **essential** for proper fit. Before beginning your project, make a sample swatch in the yarn and needle or hook specified. After completing the swatch, measure it, counting your stitches and rows/rounds carefully. If your swatch is larger or smaller than specified, **make another, changing hook size to get the correct gauge**. Keep trying until you find the size needle or hook that will give you the specified gauge.

MARKERS

Knit: As a convenience to you, we have used markers to help distinguish the beginning of a pattern or round. Place markers as instructed. You may use purchased markers or tie a length of contrasting color yarn around the needle. When you reach a marker on each row or round, slip it from the left needle to the right needle; remove it when no longer needed.

Crochet: Markers are used to help distinguish the beginning of each round being worked. Place a 2" (5 cm) scrap piece of yarn before the first stitch of each round, moving the marker after each round is complete.

KNITTING IN THE ROUND

Circular Needle

When you knit a tube, you are going to work around on the outside of the circle, with the **right** side of the knitting facing you.

Using a circular needle, cast on all stitches as instructed. Untwist and straighten the stitches on the needle to be sure that the cast on ridge lays on the inside of the needle and never rolls around the needle.

Hold the needle so that the skein of the yarn is attached to the stitch closest to the right-hand point.

Place a marker on the right-hand point to mark the beginning of the round ***(Fig. 1)***.

To begin working in the round, knit the stitches on the left-hand point. Continue working each round as instructed without turning the work.

Fig. 1

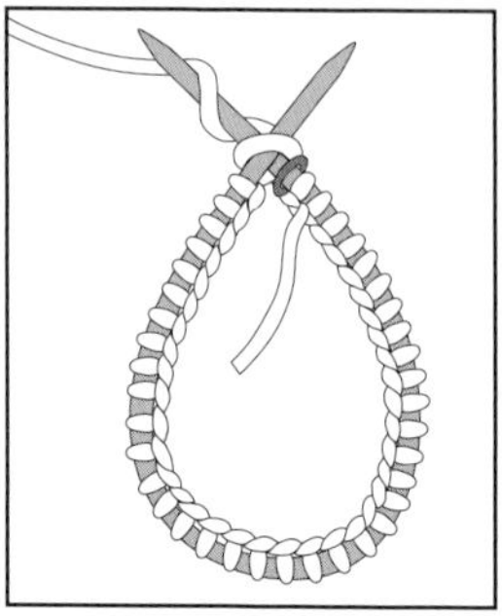

Double-Pointed Needles

When working too few stitches to use a circular needle, double-pointed needles are required. Divide the stitches between three or four double-pointed needles ***(Figs. 2a & b)***.

Fig. 2a

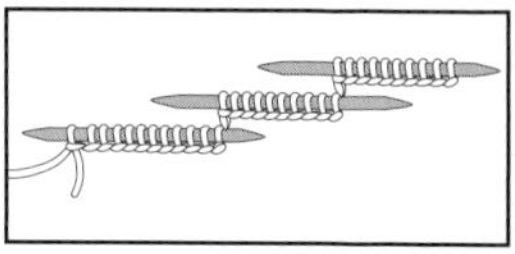

Fig. 2b

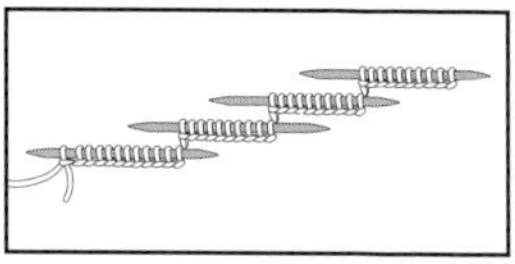

Being careful not to twist the cast on ridge, form a triangle or square with the needles ***(Figs. 2c & d)***.

Fig. 2c

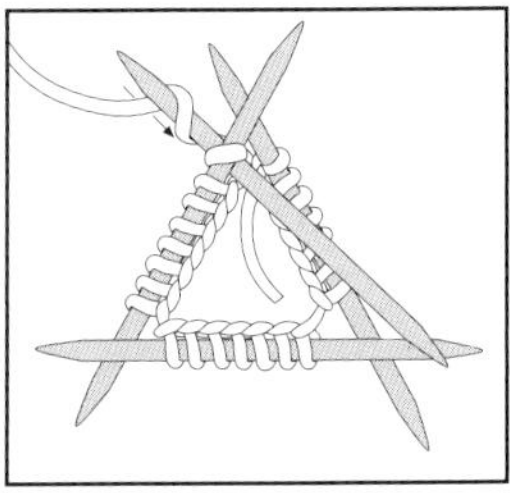

Fig. 2d

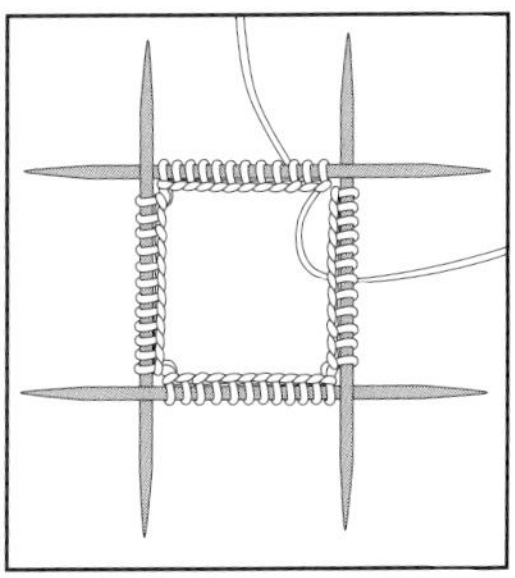

With the working yarn coming from the stitch on the last needle, work across the stitches on the first needle. You will now have an empty needle with which to work the stitches from the next needle. Work the first stitch of each needle firmly to prevent gaps. Continue working around without turning the work.

YARN OVER

Bring the yarn forward **between** the needles, then back **over** the top of the right-hand needle and forward **between** the needles again, so that it is now in position to purl the next stitch ***(Fig. 3)***.

Fig. 3

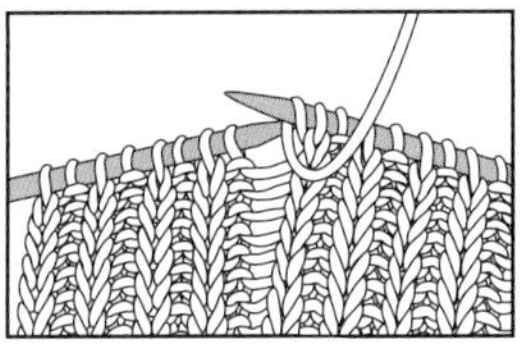

DECREASES

Knit 2 Together

(abbreviated k2tog)

Insert the right needle into the **front** of the first two stitches on the left needle as if to **knit** ***(Fig. 4)***, then **knit** them together as if they were one stitch.

Fig. 4

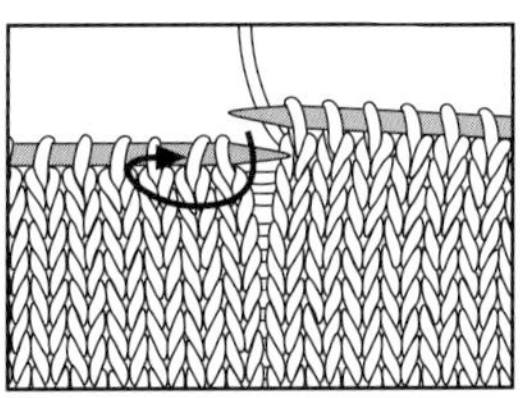

Purl 2 Together

(abbreviated p2tog)
Insert the right needle into the **front** of the first two stitches on the left needle as if to **purl** ***(Fig. 5)***, then **purl** them together as if they were one stitch.

Fig. 5

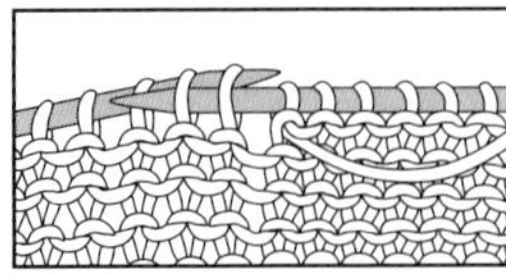

Slip, Slip, Knit

(abbreviated SSK)
With the yarn in back of work, separately slip two stitches as if to knit ***(Fig. 6a)***. Insert the left needle into the **front** of both slipped stitches ***(Fig. 6b)*** and **knit** them together as if they were one stitch ***(Fig. 6c)***.

Fig. 6a

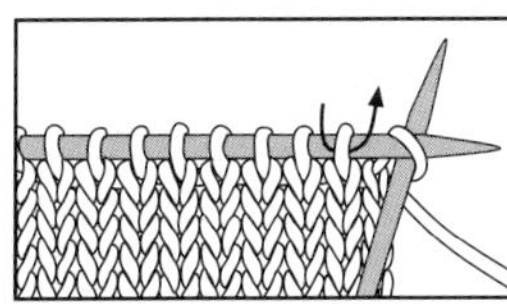

Fig. 6b

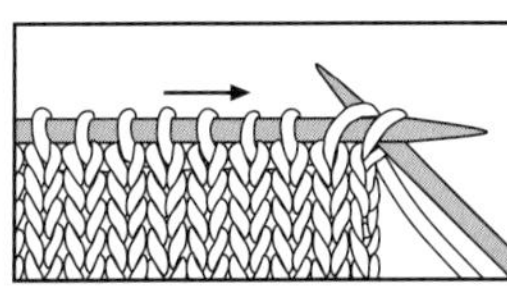

Fig. 6c

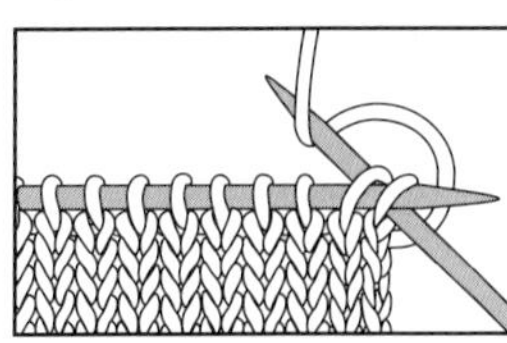

Double Crochet 2 Together

(abbreviated dc2tog)
(uses next 2 sts)
* Yarn over, insert hook in **next** st, yarn over and pull up a loop, yarn over and draw through 2 loops on hook; repeat from * once **more**, yarn over and draw through all 3 loops on hook ***(Figs. 7a & b)***.

Fig. 7a

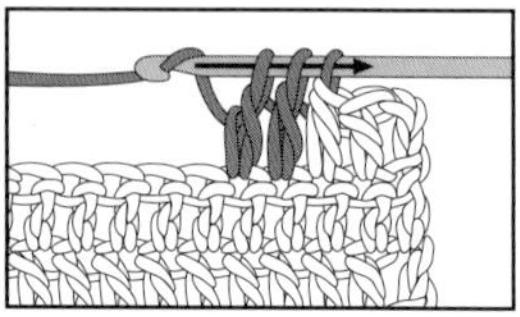

Fig. 7b

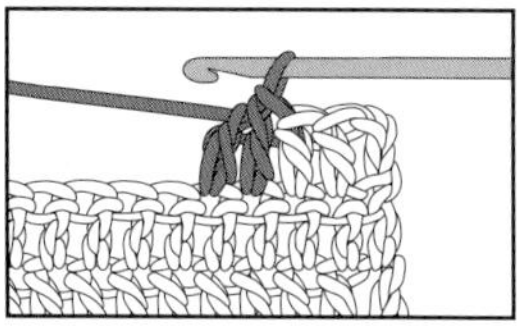

BACK LOOP ONLY

Work only in loop(s) indicated by arrow ***(Fig. 8)***.

Fig. 8

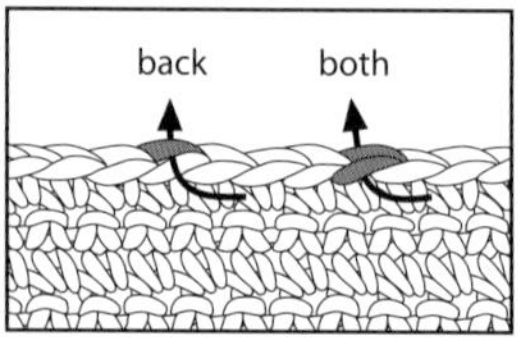

POST STITCH

Work around post of stitch indicated, inserting hook in direction of arrow ***(Fig. 9)***.

Fig. 9

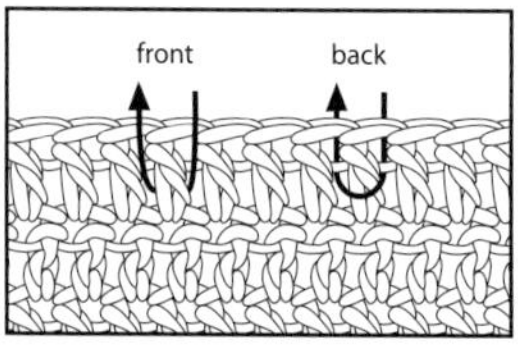

CHANGING COLORS

Work the last stitch to within one step of completion, hook new yarn ***(Fig. 10)*** and draw through both loops on hook.

Fig. 10

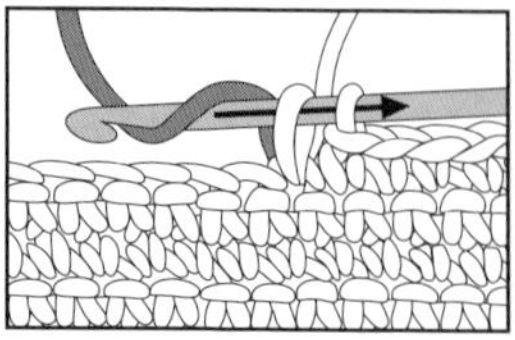

WORKING IN SPACE BEFORE A STITCH

When instructed to work in space **before** a stitch or in spaces **between** stitches, insert hook in space indicated by arrow ***(Fig. 11)***.

Fig. 11

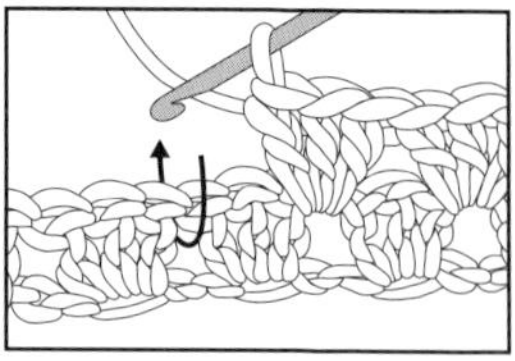

We have made every effort to ensure that these instructions are accurate and complete. We cannot, however, be responsible for human error, typographical mistakes, or variations in individual work.

Made in U.S.A.